Whitewash/Blackwash

Myths of the Viet Nam War

by Bill Laurie and R. J. Del Vecchio

Bill Laurie has degrees in Political Science and Economics, and a secondary education teaching certificate, having completed the coursework for an Education degree. He served in Viet Nam as a US Army Intelligence Officer at MACV J-2 in Saigon, with periodic assignments in the Mekong delta, and was also OIC of a unit Civic Action/MEDCAP project from 1971-1972. He returned to Viet Nam from 1973-1975 as a Defense Department intelligence analyst and liaison contact with RVN Armed Forces, with whom he often worked directly. Since then, Mr. Laurie has continued research about the war, its underlying causes and its conduct, and interviewed scores of Southeast Asian veterans, both US- and Southeast Asian-born. He is currently completing a thoroughly documented study illustrating how the conflict in SE Asia has been profoundly distorted in America's collective historical view.

R. J. Del Vecchio has a BS & MS in Chemistry, which somehow caused the Marine Corps to assign him the Photography MOS after basic training. After instruction in military photography in Quantico, VA and Ft Monmouth, NJ, and service in the Quantico Photographic Services Lab, he volunteered to go to Viet Nam. He spent from December '67 to November '68 as a Combat Photographer for the 1st Marine Division. A number of his photographs are in the National Archives in College Park, MD, and one of his Nikon cameras is in the Marine Corps museum, displaying a bullet hole through its frame. He has been active in various veterans' groups and regularly gives presentations on Viet Nam in high schools and colleges. He has been a consultant in a technical field for 16 years, and has previously authored books on applied Polymer Science and industrial applications of statistical methods.

Bill Laurie and R. J. Del Vecchio

(available at TechConsultServ@Juno.com)

Credits

We wish to acknowledge the help and inspiration provided by many people, who have worked selflessly for decades to preserve and illuminate the historical truths of the conflict in SouthEast Asia. We cannot hope to say enough to recognize and honor all those who struggled and suffered and sacrificed there, but this booklet is dedicated to their memory. May those who fell rest in peace, those who returned find peace, and those in SE Asia who still yearn for freedom be able someday to achieve it.

Special thanks for the contributions of Mike Benge, Jim McLeroy, and Steve Sherman.

Historically significant stamps courtesy of the Radix Foundation

Cover photographs from USMC Combat Photographers

This work was underwritten totally by contributions from individual veterans and veterans' organizations, including

North Carolina Vietnam Veterans, Inc.

Cover Art

Front Cover- Images from 1967-68

From upper left to right, then down and left to right again

1. May 1968- Marines assaulting an NVA machinegun nest during an intense battle on Goi Noi Island
2. Christmas 1967- VN children at a Marine holiday party for village children, near Da Nang
3. Early February 1968- Marines returning to base after a battle in the mountains inland from Da Nang
4. Late February 1968- a flame tank in operation during the battle of Hue
5. September 1968- Marines providing medical aid to villagers during a peaceful sweep of their area
6. September 1968 (a day later)- a Marine machinegun team during a firefight with NVA

Back Cover- Stamps of Historical Significance

From upper left to right, then down and left to right again

1. 1955 SVN stamp commemorating the exodus of as many as 1MM people from the North to the South in 1954; a precursor to the "boat people" of 1975-80
2. 1960 NVN stamp honoring "Uncle Ho"
3. 1965 NVN issue celebrating a US antiwar protestor and his supporters
4. 1967 NVN image of a US POW, shown as a hulking prisoner of a small VN woman
5. 1968 NVN issue demonstrating solidarity with communist revolutionaries across the world
6. 1969 SVN stamp depicting communist atrocities committed during the 1968 Tet Offensive
7. 1966 Cuban stamp accusing the US of genocide in Viet Nam by use of poison gas
8. 1972 SVN stamp celebrating the defeat by ARVN forces of a major invasion by the NVA early that year
9. 1970 PRG issue honoring Lenin and associating him with the Viet Cong flag
10. 1970 SVN stamp depicting the rebuilding of war damage inflicted during the Tet Offensive

CONTENTS

Foreword

The creation of myths is a normal occurrence in history, fueled by various factors ranging from romanticism (e.g. Camelot) to deliberate, purposeful manipulation (Aryans as ubermenschen destined to rule others). Misinformation/misperceptions can grow into myths over time, and if irresponsible, biased journalism is practiced, a myth can sprout and flower readily. Press coverage of the Indian wars supported the myth of the ignorant savage and contributed heavily to their unfair treatment by the US government.

Some myths are harmless or lose meaning over time, others still have effects at varying levels. For instance, there is an often-accepted myth that the United States won WW2, or at least, was the single major contributor to the defeat of the Axis powers. However, the historical fact is that 8 out of 10 German soldiers who died in the war died on the Russian front. There is no doubt that America's contribution in materiel to the UK and Russia was of great value, and that American military power swung the balance in the end, so the myth is relatively harmless, but it is a myth, not historical reality.

It is also possible for myths to grow to the point of overshadowing the historical reality, especially if writers and educators reinforce and spread them. False myths can ultimately have significant negative impact on a society. This has become the case for the many myths relating to the conflict in Southeast Asia over the years 1954-1980; while the primary focus is usually America's involvement in Viet Nam, there are many other important dimensions to the situation in the region at the time.

After 1975, many veterans of Viet Nam tended to withdraw from discussions and even thoughts about the war. The myths of the war were growing, but either from avoidance or from making the assumption that they would fade away, veterans did not often address them publicly or privately. Now, however, it has become clear that their continued and relatively unchallenged growth has created significant problems and difficulties for this country. Therefore it is from a sense of duty to both our brothers and others who suffered and died because of the war, as well as our concern for the future of our country's struggles in an increasingly complex and threatening world, that these authors and other contributors are compelled to clarify and expose at least some of the major myths that have been accepted as historical fact.

As with any significant sustained conflict, any attempt to provide a detailed historical examination of even a limited aspect of the war would require many volumes. This will be a very basic treatment of a selected group of myths, deliberately concise and readable, with a minimum of academic trappings. It is our intent to demonstrate how fallacious the chosen ideas are, provide an ample list of reference works for those who wish to investigate in more depth, and help readers understand that the many other myths not addressed here are equally subject to examination and critical review.

It is time, and more than time, to set the record straight. There are plenty of valid aspects of the conflict that can be discussed/debated from differing points of view, without wasting time or clouding the discussions trying to deal with demonstrably erroneous and seriously misleading myths. Proper understanding of history equips a society to react better to evolving situations and challenges, as opposed to the continuation of mistaken policies based on false history. Maintaining the specious myths of Viet Nam has become a luxury (as well as an injustice) that this nation can no longer afford.

Introduction

War is the most terrible human experience, the most critical action possible, the most confusing phenomenon known, No major historical event, such as a war of any length, can ever be made fully comprehensible by any one book, or even by a series of books. The American Civil War has been the subject of millions of hours of research by myriad historians over the past 140 years. Thousands of books have been written, including series of volumes from a single source that attempted to provide a broad view and cover all the signal events and strategies of the war. By now the judgments of history have been made about all the principal aspects of the Civil War, and yet still no one person can claim to truly know and understand the entirety of what happened, no matter how many of those books they have read.

This booklet will only provide an extremely condensed overview of the war in Viet Nam and certainly cannot even remotely approach a thorough treatment of that history. Its primary purpose is to illustrate with a limited number of examples how the commonly accepted psuedohistory of the conflict is riddled with errors and misinformation. Many substantial volumes are available which the interested reader can examine for the detailed history.[1] The purpose of this small volume is to give that reader a much better chance of detecting and discounting the biased/inaccurate/erroneous elements to be found in many of those reference works.

---

[1] The primary database for this book was the lengthy reference work on the war by Mr. Laurie, which will be available in 2006.

Section 1- Background and Prologue

Myth #1- The US had no reason to be involved in Viet Nam

The Cold War, a face-off between the Western powers and Soviet-based Communism, erupted into view shortly after the end of World War Two, and ended with the collapse of the Soviet Union in 1991. It is not easy for those who did not live in those times to understand the degree of concern that gripped the United States and many other countries during the 1950s and early 1960s. A long list of countries[2] had been taken over by communists, using subterfuge, destabilization, and outright force, and the stated aim of international communism was to achieve world domination. A premier of Russia pounded a table in the UN and proclaimed to the American public "We will bury you!" With the Soviet bloc right on the borders of Europe, and China threatening Asia, the vision of a world possibly overrun by the Reds seemed all too real; and the reports from refugees of what life under Communism was like were more than enough to make Americans anxious to prevent that vision from ever coming true.

The primary strategy of the US was the Containment Policy, whereby the US and its allies would do everything possible to prevent the continued takeover of countries by Communism. It was hoped/believed that over time the communist system would fall prey to inherent flaws and eventually fall apart. Communist insurgencies in Greece, Malaysia, Indonesia, and parts of South America were defeated, and South Korea was freed from the invasion

---

[2] Estonia, Latvia, Lithuania, Poland, Hungary, Romania, Bulgaria, Czechoslovakia, East Germany, China, etc.

by the communist North in a bloody war supported primarily by American troops.[3]

Early in John F. Kennedy's presidency a crisis arose with a communist threat of missiles based in Cuba. This was resolved by brinkmanship diplomacy, but it served to maintain the resolve of the US to support the Containment Policy. Thus the threat of communists taking over all of Viet Nam, which America had become well aware of during the 1954 division of that country as the French abandoned their imperial policy, was seen as the next incursion of expansionist Communism. And logically, the next place where every means had to be brought to bear to limit that incursion. The possibility that the other countries of SE Asia would then suffer communist subversion and eventual takeover was called the Domino Theory.

While arguments have been made that the situation might have been handled differently, the resistance to the spread of Communism into Southeast Asia[4] was entirely consistent with Containment. Therefore, it is a myth that the USA had no stake in Viet Nam, no real interest in the conflict.

Myth #2- Ho Chi Minh was a nationalist and a benevolent leader of his people

There has been a great deal of publicity about the central figure of North Viet Nam (NVN), known best by

---

[3] The atrocities committed by the communist troops, insincere and manipulative negotiations by the North Koreans, and horrific treatment of POWs were all aspects of communist actions that foreshadowed Viet Nam.

[4] Since Laos and Cambodia share borders with Viet Nam, and also border on Thailand, which borders on Malaysia, the avenues for the possible spread of communism across the region were obvious.

the name Ho Chi Minh.[5] He is usually depicted as a kindly old man, but with a lifelong history as a nationalist struggling to free his homeland from the French. However, in fact he left Viet Nam in 1912 to live in France, where he became a founding member of the French Communist Party. Later he lived in Russia, where he attended the Lenin Institute to be trained as a professional revolutionary. "Uncle Ho" only returned to Viet Nam in 1941 for a brief visit, did not actually take up residence there again until 1944.

The record of his activities shows him to have been a devoted communist first and a nationalist second. And like the Bolsheviks who took over the Russian Revolution from all the other political groups fighting the czarists, the Vietnamese communists, under Ho's leadership, carefully eliminated all the purely nationalist groups who had fought the French. A variety of means, including betraying them to the French, direct violent action, and "disappearing" individuals and groups, were used by the communists over the years.[6]

After the division of the country in 1954 and full takeover of the North by the communists, the imposition of a communist system there was marked by brutality and injustice, and sparked various levels of resistance. An estimated 60,000 people were killed in the so-called "land reform" between 1954 and 1956. In Ho's home province of Nghe An a farmer's rebellion broke out in September 1956. He dispatched a full army division to suppress it, and up to 6,000 people were killed or deported as a result. Years earlier Ho had made a brief and pointed comment on how he regarded all forms of dissent- "All

---

[5] This was not his birth name, in fact he used several names at various times in his life, but settled on Ho Chi Minh (he who enlightens) as an effective enhancement of his public image.

[6] Ho was no stranger to such tactics, having betrayed a famous nationalist leader (Phan Boi Chau) to the French many years before.

those who do not follow the line that I have set out will be smashed."

Despite all the heavy propaganda depicting Ho Chi Minh as a kindly, long-suffering, and heroic patriot, this image is also a myth. He was a clever, unprincipled, dedicated communist first and foremost, given to the brutal practices he had studied at the Lenin Institute.[7]

Myth #3- The South Vietnamese government denied the people a free election on unification

Another commonly held position is that the communists in the South had every right to continue the guerrilla warfare there (and the North had every right to support them with men and materiel), since the government of South Viet Nam (SVN) refused to hold free elections called for by the Geneva Accords; which were the diplomatic tool by which the French left the country and the opposing Vietnamese factions were to settle things.

In reality, neither the US nor the Diem government of SVN had signed the Accords, which were actually drawn up between the French and the Viet Minh. In addition, only the Final Declaration drafted in Geneva called for elections, and no one signed that document. Thus it is entirely a myth that the South Vietnamese had any obligation to set up or take part in elections connected to political parties in the North.[8]

It is worth noting that the Accords were in fact violated by one of the signing parties, the government of Ho Chi Minh. On the one hand they did not allow free flow of

---

[7] Ho considered Lenin a superhero and hoped to meet him in the afterlife.

[8] Of which there was effectively only one, the Communist Party; the numerous other nationalist groups who'd fought the French had been decimated by then.

people wishing to leave the North[9], and on the other hand did not require all the remaining Viet Minh agents to leave the South. Both of these had been principal elements in the Articles of the Accords.

Myth #4- The Viet Cong were an idealistic nationalist group, just like the American Minutemen

Numerous sources have compared the Viet Cong (direct successors to the Viet Minh, focussed on overthrowing the government of the South as the Viet Minh had focussed on overthrowing the French) and the American Minutemen. In this view, the Viet Cong (VC) were independent nationalists fighting to depose an illegitimate and universally detested puppet government that was thwarting the will of the people to be united with NVN and its communist government.

However, none of the elements of this argument stand up to objective consideration. First, the government of SVN, seriously imperfect as it was, was certainly no more illegitimate than the government of NVN, where the general population never had any chance to vote one way or another, but had the communist government imposed on them.

Secondly, given the lack of any mass migration of ordinary citizens from the South to the North during partition, and the major migration from the North to the South at that time, clearly the bulk of the southern population did not detest their government nor have a burning desire to come under communist rule.

---

[9] About 900,000 people did manage to flee to the South (often with major hardships and difficulties), at least 300,000 more were prevented from leaving.

Thirdly, while many of the rank and file VC were politically unschooled and generally nationalistic rather than communist, they took their orders from the Marxist political cadre of the former Viet Minh, who were all under the direct control of the North. They were really an extension of the power of the North, not an independent movement arising spontaneously from the general population of the South.[10]

Yet the most telling facts about the VC were the strategies and tactics they employed. While they did on occasion attack the military and governmental centers of SVN, the bulk of their efforts went to destabilize the whole society by means of brutal terrorism. They targeted village chiefs, policemen, schoolteachers, agricultural aid workers, and other government employees. Abductions, assassinations, and bombings were daily events, and often the murders were public and deliberately horrific (impalings on long bamboo shafts, for example, in which the victim dies slowly in great agony) to drive terror deep into the minds of the witnesses.

In the period 1957-67 there were between 25,000 to 35,000 assassinations/abductions[11], a substantial total for a country with a population of about 16 million. After 1968 people were killed or disappeared at a lower rate, due to the damage the VC organization suffered during and after Tet, but the murders continued. This is terrorism on a large scale, and if the practice of the VC was to liquidate those who opposed them, this total indicates clearly a very substantial level of the population opposed them; but if they were killing people who did not oppose them, then they were indiscriminate murderers.

---

[10] Of the sincere nationalists among the NLF/VC, some eventually ended up in Paris as refugees from the communists.

[11] Since only a tiny fraction of those abducted ever returned, it as assumed the rest were killed.

Either way, there are no parallels whatsoever with the way Americans fought our revolution and the concept of the VC as Minutemen is a particularly bizarre myth.

Myth #5- The rationale for US intervention in Viet Nam was based on a fraud

American military advisors had been supporting the South Vietnamese from the late 1950s, but no regular US military units were in the country until 1965. The triggering event[12] for committing conventional forces to the direct support of SVN was the attack by the North Vietnamese on US Navy destroyers in the Gulf of Tonkin that August. Three attacks were reported, two on the *Maddox* and one on the *Turner Joy*.

Much has been made of the lack of hard evidence of any attack on the *Turner Joy* or the second attack on the *Maddox*. Antiwar activists later made sweeping claims that no attacks ever occurred, that Lyndon Johnson was somehow involved in a conspiracy to defraud the American public in order to justify intervention in Viet Nam. However, there were bullet holes in the *Maddox* from the first attack, public statements were made by NVN proclaiming a supposed victory in chasing the *Maddox* from their coastal waters, and after the war a torpedo tube was displayed at the Hanoi War Museum, which was proudly identified as being from one of the boats that attacked the US Navy in the Bay of Tonkin. These facts demonstrate that this "conspiracy" is also a myth.

---

[12] There had already been a series of fatal assaults in SVN on Americans, including bombings at the US embassy and at a US Officers' Club; President Johnson considered the Gulf of Tonkin attacks the final straw.

Section 2- Progression of Events

Myth #6- The US military routinely used inhumane tactics on the people, while the VC were benefactors

During the initial direct US involvement in the war there was considerable support by the public and in the press. The plight of the refugees from the North, the atrocities committed by the VC, and the desire of many Southerners to defeat the VC and remain independent of the North were covered in the media on a regular basis. However, as time went on the publicity given to the negative aspects of the conflict grew steadily, starting perhaps with a famous scene in which US Marines set fire to a village using their Zippo lighters. Stories of mistreatment of prisoners by US and South Vietnamese forces began to surface, and articles appeared in the Western press by members of the National Liberation Front (NLF), the puppet organization of the North Vietnamese government that supposedly represented the pure nationalist movement in SVN.

There have always been fervent antiwar people in the US (even after Pearl Harbor one congressperson still wouldn't vote for war), and they became steadily more active. The 1960s were a time of major social debates, and on school campuses there was a steady increase in student involvement in numerous humanistic causes, such as women's rights, racial equality, and general questioning of, and mistrust in, authority. Antiwar activities very naturally became a part of this movement.

While the bulk of the originating professors, students, and other peace activists were sincere idealists, the movement soon attracted its share of radicals, who were more vocal, more exciting, and more newsworthy than the moderates. Some were clearly leftist sympathizers with a very strong antigovernment agenda. As the casualty lists from Viet Nam grew and reports of failed strategies, corruption in the government of SVN, and incompetence in the military forces of SVN became more and more common in the media, the antiwar movement gained in strength and stridency.

One of the tactics of the more radical activists was to glorify the VC and NVN while finding any and all reasons to denigrate the South Vietnamese and US actions. Stories abounded of the unnecessary destruction wreaked by American troops, brutal treatment of innocent villagers, routine use of torture and secret assassinations by Americans (often attributed to the CIA but also to various elements of the military). At the same time a great deal of emphasis was given to portrayals of the VC as Minutemen (referenced above), and the kindly "Uncle Ho", who was portrayed as leading a unified society committed one and all to the liberation of their brothers in the South. The North knew very well how to use propaganda. (The imprisonments or disappearances of all Northerners who offered the slightest opposition to the war were never brought to light until long after it was over.)

Many sincere (and sometimes naïve) people in the US and elsewhere fell into believing only the good reports about the VC and the NVN government, and only the bad reports about the SVN government, American policies, and actions of US soldiers. Since there are always mistakes made in the conduct of any war, and at least some bad behavior on the part of combat troops and others in the theater of war[13], some of the reports of bad behavior by Americans were valid. This was taken in general as proof that all such reports were accurate and

[13] Dozens of US soldiers were hung during WW2 for rape, and there were a few instances of executions of captured SS deathcamp guards, etc.

precise, and that such behavior was typical of US troops, and directed by military policy.

However, the real facts are that US troops committed few heinous acts, all by individuals or small groups as matters of exception, and when discovered, people were often prosecuted for it. There was no policy of murder and purposeless destruction by the US military (although wars have always brought massive levels of destruction), nor were VC and North Vietnamese Army (NVA, also referred to as PAVN, Peoples' Army of Vietnam) POWs badly treated in general.

In contrast, assassinations were a major tactic of the VC (see above), and the treatment of POWs by the communists was consistently brutal.[14] The most dramatic evidence of the murderous cruelty of the communists was the deliberate collection and slaughter of 3000-6000 people in Hue when the NVA succeeded in taking over most of the city for a few days during the Tet Offensive of 1968. Lists of those slated for liquidation had been carefully prepared in advance; such death lists also existed for other cities, and only the lack of success in taking over other areas in SVN prevented their being implemented.

For those who have not studied war, it is easy to be appalled by events that are actually a common (yet certainly tragic) part of the horror of war. Soldiers in the midst of combat don't always take prisoners, nor exercise perfect judgment about what level of violence is justified at every moment. Long-term stress, both physical and psychological, takes a heavy toll that often leaves soldiers numbed and/or reflexively defensive/aggressive. Nor do military recruiting and training screen out the

---

[14] The permanent injuries resulting from prolonged torture evident on the bodies of surviving US POWs back up their stories of barbaric mistreatment.

small fraction of any population that is susceptible to overreaction and excessive violence. In any war, the occurrence of a limited number of criminal incidents is not justification for shock and surprise; indeed, it is the absence of any such incidents that would be miraculous. Even a few events as immoral and appalling as My Lai[15] cannot justify blanket condemnation of one party's entire conduct of the conflict. Only by a consistent pattern of acts that reveal a policy can any judgment be made.

The consistent use of terrorism, torture, duplicity, and murder made by the communist forces during the war clearly reveals their conscious policies and the character of their leaders. The whitewash of the long, deep history of their brutality[16] and the simultaneous "blackwash" of American actions led to the truly detestable myth of "Americans = bad guys, VC/NVA = good guys".

Myth #7- The Tet Offensive was a devastating blow to the US and SVN forces and a major military victory for the communists

US involvement in the war climbed steadily from 1965 and the peak of American combat experience was reached in 1968; in that year over 14,500 Americans died in Viet Nam and almost 48,000 were wounded.

The Lunar New Year celebration, known as Tet, is the biggest holiday in Vietnamese culture, and there had been a truce between the opposing forces every year since the partitioning of the country. In 1968 the communists decided to launch a masterstroke offensive

---

[15] It should be noted there was an investigation and a court-martial connected to My Lai, and that the US military conducted numerous other war crimes investigations and sentenced soldiers to prison in many cases; there were no trials by the communists of any of their people who'd committed atrocities.

[16] E.g., a horrid massacre at Dak Son, in which 252 Montagnard villagers were burned to death by NVA flamethrowers, is essentially unknown to the public.

planned by their famous general Vo Nguyen Giap; he was the mastermind of the 1954 battle of Dien Bien Phu, which was the final decisive victory over the French forces and led to the Geneva Accords.

In order to absolutely maximize the element of surprise, Giap chose to schedule the attack during Tet truce, when about half of the South Vietnamese military would be home on leave and those remaining on duty, plus the Americans, would not be expecting anything to happen. The plan was to completely shock the defending forces, overrun them as they panicked and ran, and inspire a general uprising of South Vietnamese sympathizers that would reinforce the VC and NVA and enable them to take and hold significant portions of the country. This would be the beginning of the end, the Americans would lose all heart and abandon South Vietnam, the SVN government would fall apart, and complete victory for the communists would follow.

Men and supplies were smuggled into many cities, careful preparations were made, and NVA units moved into positions for their assaults. As Tet began, well-coordinated attacks took place all over Viet Nam, mainly by hard-core VC units in some places, but often by NVA units in conjunction with VC guides and infiltrators.

Battles of various magnitudes went on for several days, dramatic scenes took place such as the failed attack on the US embassy in Saigon, and in Hue the surrounded US military HQ known as the MACV compound, that held out against all odds like a replay of the Alamo. The nightly news in the US was full of scenes of destruction, house-to-house fighting, bodies lying on the streets, and reports from clearly frightened newspeople in flak jackets and helmets, speaking of waves of attackers and the uncertainty of the outcome. The confusion and fear that are the absolute norm of combat situations were communicated with crystal clarity to the American public. Since the great majority was unfamiliar with the harsh realities of war, they were naturally horrified and dismayed by the graphic images on their TV screens. This led to an extremely heightened level of anxiety and pessimism among many, which was not relieved by the actual results of the communist offensive.

By February 25 the last major action related to the attack (the clearing of NVA from Hue) was over, and not a single one of the communist objectives had been met. During that initial major phase of the offensive, the South Vietnamese military sustained about 6,000 casualties, and the US forces under 2,000. In the same period the VC/NVA losses were 20,000+ (of ~80,000 for the year). The soldiers of the South, who mounted the defenses in the majority of the targeted areas, not only refused to break and run, they fought bravely and smashed most of the VC/NVA units they encountered. Also, there was no popular uprising against the government, and the bulk of the South Vietnamese reacted strongly against the appalling violation of the truce and the slaughter of civilians by the communists. This change in attitude resulted in the enlistments in the SVN military shooting up very dramatically in the months after Tet.

Militarily, Tet was an unmitigated disaster for the communist forces, as was confirmed years later by the former NVA colonel[17] who had received the formal surrender of South Viet Nam in 1975. The VC took so many casualties that they lost the great bulk of their effectiveness and never recovered as a strategic fighting force. Communist credibility with the population of the South was badly damaged, and their ability to recruit new VC fighters declined markedly. At the same time, the

---

[17] Bui Tin, who had been on the NVA general staff, and later became editor of the People's Daily, the official newspaper of Viet Nam.

morale and determination of the South Vietnamese military were enormously improved.

This would, to an objective military strategist, add up to very possibly being the beginning of the end for the communist attempt to conquer the South. And in fact the SVN military grew steadily better in strength and skill from that time on, which made possible the full implementation of "Vietnamization"[18] of the war in 1970-72. The view that the Tet offensive was in any remote sense a communist military victory is basically absurd, yet it has been one of the more prevalent myths of the war.

Myth #8- Media coverage of the war was balanced and accurate and contributed to development of appropriate US policies

However, the overriding effect of the Tet offensive in the US was extremely damaging psychologically; at the least it convinced many people that the outcome of the conflict was in severe doubt, and at the worst it absolutely confirmed to many others that it was an unwinnable war, or that the US leadership had been deceiving people about the progress made, or both.

Perhaps the pivotal event of the time was a broadcast on February 27th by Walter Cronkite, the greatly respected dean of US newsmen, after his return from visiting the war zone. Although he had previously been at least tacitly supportive of the war, and been reasonably objective in his reporting, in the dramatic TV spot late that February he was strongly negative about what had happened and the general prospects for the future of the war. Some of his statements were clearly in error, he

---

[18] This was the takeover of full responsibility for all areas of SVN by the armed forces of SVN, and the departure of US forces, as outlined by Pres. Nixon.

made some predictions that failed to come true, and he wound up declaring the war a "stalemate" that could only be settled by negotiation.

Cronkite was not an expert in military matters or international politics, and he began the address noting it was a "speculative, personal, subjective" commentary, so his remarks could and should have been received as what they were: one man's feelings and perceptions of a complex situation, heavily colored by the confusion and destruction he had just witnessed. However, his popularity and prestige were such that his words were taken by many as a definitive analysis of the situation, and the already existing antiwar movement capitalized on the impact of his broadcast. Lyndon Johnson's despairing comment about the broadcast was "If I've lost Cronkite, I've lost middle America."

From an historical point of view, this was like a reporter returning from Europe right after the Battle of the Bulge and telling the American people that the ability of the Germans to launch this large surprise attack and cause so much destruction, demonstrated that we'd have to negotiate with Hitler to end the war. The belief that Mr. Cronkite, and other reporters after him, provided valid inputs on the war situation that led to good decisions about its conduct is a very tragic myth.[19]

Myth #9- Antiwar protests shortened the war and saved lives

However, the February broadcast was a precisely defined psychological turning point in the war, not only because of the effect on the general population, but

---

[19] Not only did the media provide inaccurate and biased reporting of negative events, they also failed to report at all on many positive events; such as the successful SVN land reform, a major increase of rice production, and the Chieu Hoi program, which resulted in about 200,000 defections from the VC.

especially because, as other newspeople have said, Cronkite's conversion to subjective, antiwar reporting made it not only OK but even trendy to do so. That is when the practice of media "whitewash/blackwash" really took off, with the resulting enormous boost to the antiwar movement and the steady progression of negative feelings about the war and those who were fighting it.

As 1968 went on, the civil unrest built to previously unknown heights, the Rev. Martin Luther King Jr. and Robert Kennedy were assassinated, and various riots broke out related to the antiwar and civil rights movements, culminating in several days of large-scale violent disturbances surrounding the 1968 Democratic National Convention in Chicago. Condemnation of police and government agencies dealing with the riots was widespread, and fueled more passion amongst the war protesters.

This passion led to increasing levels of disdain for, and sometimes abuse of, the military in general and returning Viet Nam veterans in particular. While the number of truly egregious actions against individual soldiers (spitting, physical harassment, public name-calling) was not high, they were reported widely enough to make everyone aware of them. That, plus the general feeling of unpopularity/disapproval experienced by most soldiers and veterans, contributed to their sense of rejection and alienation. A limited number[20] of disaffected veterans joined the antiwar movement, reinforcing its claim to the moral high ground.

The North Vietnamese government paid close attention to all of this, listening every day to world news on the radio, tracking the progress of the antiwar

---

[20] Given that over 2,500,000 men served in-country, if only 1 in 1000 turned to radical politics, it would more than account for as many or even more antiwar veterans than have ever been verified.

movement. They considered the antiwar movement essential to their strategy and rejoiced in visits to Hanoi by American public figures condemning the US involvement. They acknowledged privately that Tet had been a staggering defeat, but took heart from realizing that they had gained a political advantage, as shown so clearly by Johnson's decision to not run for office again. At that point they became supremely confident that all they had to do was maintain a level of conflict in SVN long enough and the US would pull out, not because of lack of ability to wage the war, but because steady erosion of the will to fight would force an eventual withdrawal.[21]

There were North Vietnamese, even among the Communist Party, who were not prepared to face a long conflict of doubtful outcome. The economic price of the war was very high, only sustainable through the massive aid from China and the Soviet Bloc, and the enormous losses of men were traumatizing their society.[22] Even though their dissent was not tolerated by Ho Chi Minh (see above), had he and the rest of the communist leadership been sure they were facing a resolute US, they were prepared to reconsider the continuation of the war. There are numerous grateful references to the contribution of the American antiwar movement throughout the body of NVN works on the war, and in their war museums there are even pictures of Americans credited for their help. There is no real question that the communists valued the US antiwar movement as a major ally in the war.

---

[21] All these points are made by several N. Vietnamese figures in books, memoirs, and interviews.

[22] The official NVN figure for KIA in the war is 1.1MM; an additional 300,000 are reported as missing (and presumed dead); this amounts to perhaps 1/3 the North Vietnamese men in the age group for military service.

That being the case, it is not possible to claim with any certainty that antiwar activities shortened the war or saved any lives. In fact, it is much more logical to assume the opposite, since the war very conceivably could have started winding down in 1968 as NVN started withdrawing their remaining troops; then there would not have been battles ongoing in-country through 1975, nor would the deaths of so many Vietnamese and others[23] in the aftermath of the takeover of the South have occurred.

It became a very comfortable thing to believe that the withdrawal from SVN had been the right thing for America, which all work and sacrifice of the antiwar groups had achieved the good things they desired. Nonetheless, the supposed shortening of the war and saving of lives due to that work and sacrifice are unfortunately also a myth.[24]

Myth #10- The great majority of villagers were VC sympathizers, so no counterinsurgency programs ever succeeded

The war had to be fought on many fronts; from classic battles like Hue City, to counterguerrilla tactics and jungle warfare, to counterinsurgency programs intended to cut off local aid to the VC/NVA by promoting and supporting the security and self-defensive capability of villages. This last activity was part of "winning the hearts and minds" of the people of the land, and is a classic tactic against guerrillas.

It was often claimed by the communists, and echoed by the antiwar movement, that the majority of South

---

[23] Ultimately Hanoi's sponsorship of communist movements in Laos and Cambodia was the cause of millions of deaths in those countries.

[24] Very few antiwar activists who did see what happened in Viet Nam once the communists were in power have acknowledged the falsity of this myth, and just as few newsmen of the time have admitted the anti-US bias in their reporting.

Vietnamese, and in particular those in small villages, were nationalists whose sympathies and support lay with the VC. And in fact there were some rural areas in which a substantial fraction of the population were under the sway of the VC, through a combination of misguided nationalism and psychological domination established through years of propaganda and terrorism.

However, a number of programs involving Americans and Vietnamese in joint efforts on a local level were implemented quite successfully[25] in the course of the war. These included the Special Forces camps, the Civilian Irregular Defense Group (CIDG) program, the Army's Mobile Advisory Teams, the District Advisory Teams, and the Marine Combined Action Platoons (CAP). All of these involved comparatively small numbers of Americans working closely with, and living alongside or with, local native forces.

One example of a counterinsurgency program is the CAP strategy, which involved having a small unit of Marines take up residence in a village, and work side by side with the local militia (Popular Forces or PF) in defending their area. The Marines were characterized as "Peace Corps with guns" and also worked with the Vietnamese to build houses, dig wells, provide training in medical skills, etc, and established close personal relationships with them.

At the peak, there were 114 villages in I Corps with CAP units in them. Since units were relocated when enough time, training, and experience had improved the capabilities of that village's PF to where they no longer needed the Marines, over its 5 year span the program affected a large fraction of the villages in Marine areas.

---

[25] Complaints by surviving VC commanders that after 1968 recruitment of villagers became difficult and NVA soldiers had to be used as replacements in decimated VC units demonstrate that counterinsurgency was working.

Over 5000 Marines lived and fought alongside locals during the program's life, and it proved to be effective in achieving its goals. It clearly showed that many villagers willing to fight against the VC and would form strong attachments to their Marine protectors.[26]

The Mobile Advisory Teams were closely akin to the CAP Marines, but employing even smaller units (4-5 man teams). Over 300 of these teams existed during the course of the program, which was in full swing by 1969.[27]

These examples demonstrate the falsity of the myth that all Vietnamese peasants were allies of the VC/NVA. Had that been true, the casualty rate of the thousands of Americans who were at high risk by being so exposed among the villages would have been appalling, and all these programs would have been dramatic failures. In addition, the distribution of hundreds of thousands of small arms to village defense forces after 1968 by the SVN government would never have been considered, much less implemented.

---

[26] Even 20 years after the war's end, some villages still held yearly ceremonies to honor the Marines who had fought for them.

[27] See Once A Warrior King in Recommended Reading for an account by a MAT member.

Section 3- Other Mythical Elements of the War

Myth #11- The war was fought by victims of US society, and the lasting effects on survivors were much worse than for other wars

In the later part of the war, and especially in the years immediately following the US withdrawal, it was very often stated that the average age of American soldiers was 19, that the bulk of the fighting men were drafted from the lower classes, with minimal education, and that the number of black Americans sent into battle was disproportionately high. All this was seen as clear evidence of a racist, class-conscious society using its lower elements as cannon fodder. This contributed heavily to the condemnation of the war and its leaders by elements of the Civil Rights movement.

However, the facts are:
1. the average age of men serving in Viet Nam was just over 22[28];
2. 2/3 of the those serving were volunteers, twice as many as in WW2;
3. 79% of the troops had a high school education or better, a much higher average educational level than in any other US war;
4. 12.5% of the men killed were Americans of African descent, who made up 13% of the US population at the time.

In the years after the war ended, an image of Viet Nam veterans as prone to suicide, drug use, criminal activities, and being jobless/homeless was commonly accepted. In effect, the view of them as brutal killers in a

---

[28] The average age of those killed was 23, due to pilots, career soldiers, and officers being somewhat older.

bad cause evolved into portraying them as tortured losers victimized by their involvement in a bad cause. The media went into a spiral of increasing coverage of the plight of the Viet Nam veteran. TV and movies provided characters like John Rambo, shown as a tragic figure, a dysfunctional but very dangerous survivor of the war. News crews at events where veterans were present would walk directly to those few in tattered jungle utilities and unkempt hair for interviews, bypassing the mass of those in conventional attire; the drama of the out-of-mainstream Viet Nam veteran was better for ratings, and in today's media, ratings always trump accuracy.

Examination of the facts reveals that in comparisons of bona fide Viet Nam veterans[29]:

1. their suicide rate over time has not been significantly different from the general population;
2. they make up a lower fraction of convicts than their percentage of the general population;
3. they have lower unemployment than nonveterans of their generation and no statistics prove them to make up an unusual fraction of the homeless;
4. their problems with substance abuse (drugs, alcohol) are no different than for nonveterans.

There is no question that the experience of war and combat in particular will affect people, Every combat veteran carries some effects, which can include both negative and positive elements. Every war results in some "walking wounded" coming home[30], who deserve recognition and support from the society for which they fought. The negative circumstances under which many

---

[29] The strong tendency for nonveterans in difficulties to claim veteran status has affected many poorly researched articles and studies.

[30] An Oscar-winning movie was made in 1948, dealing with the problems of returning WW2 veterans; in a more recent Oscar-winner (Saving Private Ryan) the final point of the story is that combat veterans can and do come home to lead a good life, perhaps richer and deeper in memory of their fallen comrades.

Viet Nam veterans returned home included an often abrupt transition back to civilian life, encountering various degrees of negativity towards the war and soldiers in society, and feelings of failure or hopelessness in regard to the plight of the Southeast Asians and the eventual fall of SVN. Given the commonality of these experiences, it is actually surprising that Viet Nam veterans were able in the main to readjust and lead quite normal lives.

However, the popularization of the concept of general victimhood for veterans offends the great majority of them; but sadly, it has become so pervasive that even some veterans have bought into it. It certainly has contributed to the disturbing level of phony "war heroes/victims" to be found[31], who use their supposed special status for personal glory and other gains.

This entire body of false ideas about who went to Viet Nam and in what condition they returned has been grossly unfair to both the nation and the veterans. It is a myth collection that is easily disproved by even basic research, and demonstrates the moral and professional bankruptcy of the media that created it and continue to support it.

Myth #12- The South Vietnamese never really fought well, they weren't really committed to the fight.

In the years prior to 1968 there were often reports of South Vietnamese army (ARVN) units performing very poorly in combat, the practice of buying officers' commissions was known to occur, and the political ambitions and activities of the generals were frequent matters of discussion. Many South Vietnamese were

---

[31] Numerous texts and reports deal with various aspects of these false ideas, but Stolen Valor (see Recommended Reading) is perhaps the single most complete and compelling work to deal with them.

sympathetic to the stated aims of the NLF, many held Ho Chi Minh in high regard, and many did not want to commit to the conflict one way or the other. In fact, it was the inability of the SVN government and military to react effectively to the attacks and social disruption of the VC that led the US to its steady progression of military support to the war.

However, there was slow but steady progress in improving the SVN military and the government had reached a level of stability under President Nguyen Van Thieu by 1968. The Tet Offensive had great impact on the people of SVN, for several reasons. First, the betrayal of the religious holiday truce was deeply offensive to many, and secondly, the deliberate slaughter of many victims by the communists (the terrible mass murders in Hue in particular), made it very clear just how brutal the communists forces were. People who had been sympathetic to the VC before and those who were more or less fence sitting found those positions to now be untenable, and realized that their best interests lay in the survival of SVN as an independent country.

Enlistments in the SVN military jumped dramatically, better training and weapons became available, and the quality of the entire military establishment, while still not perfect, increased substantially. As Vietnamization progressed in 1970-72 the ARVN took over the war, the proficiency of their officer corps improved, and the NVA troops in SVN continued to suffer defeats regularly.

In Spring of 1972 the North launched their most ambitious offensive, not based on myriad attacks across the country as in Tet '68, but a three-pronged conventional invasion that totaled 200,000 men, over 400 tanks, and masses of artillery.[32] They also had, for the first time, shoulder-fired surface-to-air missiles that almost nullified the use of low flying aircraft by the ARVN, which had been a critical tool for their commanders.

The fighting went on for over three months, with as many significant battles as were fought by British and American troops after D-Day on the way to Germany. In just one example of ARVN performance, the garrison at the provincial capital of An Loc, outnumbered 3 to 1 by the surrounding NVA, and subjected for months to an artillery bombardment three times as intense as was leveled against Dien Bien Phu, held out successfully, destroying 72 NVA tanks and killing about a third of the attacking force during their siege.

In the end all the invading NVA divisions were forced to withdraw from the South, having lost almost all of their tank and artillery forces, and suffering at least 80,000 KIA, easily 6-8 times the ARVN losses. This was the worst and most costly defeat the North ever suffered. The enormous advantage of the tank and superior artillery support of the NVA was offset by US bombing. Periodic difficulties notwithstanding, in the final analysis it was the skill, discipline, and determination of the South Vietnamese soldiers that denied victory to the invaders.

Three years later, during the final days of SVN, there were other incredible stands made by ARVN troops. At Xuan Loc, an ARVN division and an Airborne Brigade chewed up a superior NVA force in an intense and prolonged battle despite the enemy's massive artillery support and a clearly deteriorating military situation.

---

[32] The Russian 130mm and 122mm cannons were technically superior to even the best US made artillery available to the ARVN, and had devastating effect.

A large book could and indeed should be written about the outstanding courage and effectiveness of the South Vietnamese military in the last years of the war. But there has been little interest in such research, and the cruel and appallingly unjust myth of the poor soldiering of the South Vietnamese has gone unchallenged.

Myth #13- American POWs and other prisoners of the communists were treated humanely

Part of the antiwar movement's strategy of making the North Vietnamese the "good guys" was to reinforce the communist propaganda about their treatment of prisoners. Their self-serving reports of how POWs were treated were accepted at face value, and at various times American and other Western visitors were given special tours of the prisons. These were carefully arranged, and prisoners who did not promise to behave properly during such visits were not seen and suffered painful penalties. But these showcase tours were well publicized, and used to shore up the "nice guy" image of NVN.

The public record of communist practices with POWs is all too clear. Of the French who surrendered at Dien Bien Phu, just over a third survived their captivity.[33] Of the 559 Americans shot down in the Laotian territory almost completely controlled by the NVA, fewer than 10 were ever returned. None of the Koreans taken prisoner during the war was ever seen again. Even missionaries and civilians from the US and other countries doing humanitarian work in SVN were abducted and died in captivity.[34]

---

[33] In addition, some prisoners were never released; seven Algerian soldiers from the French forces at Dien Ben Phu escaped to Thailand 25 years later.

[34] E.g., five Germans running a medical clinic for civilians in An Hoa were taken away by the VC; only two survived to be released 5 years later; of 141 US and foreign national civilians taken prisoner during the war, only 59 were released.

Several former POWs taken prisoner in SVN have written in detail about their experiences; their descriptions of their treatment provide a consistent picture of major physical abuse and severe malnutrition, periodic deliberate torture, and some instances of deliberate execution. The survival rate of those captured in SVN is estimated to be under 50%.

The POWs shot down in NVN and held there have also written of their experiences, which involve not only poor nutrition, terrible living conditions, and general physical abuse, but very substantial levels of torture practiced on a long term basis. Many of them have permanently damaged shoulder joints from a popular torture technique using ropes to disjoint the shoulders and cause agony lasting for many hours. Their survival rate was much better, but nonetheless 113 out of 771 known to have been taken prisoner died in captivity.

Nor was there ever a comprehensive accounting by the communists of all those known to have survived being shot down in NVN, and many questions remain unanswered about what really happened to them all. Co-operation in locating remains of US servicemen has been spotty[35], and the costs of aid from the North Vietnamese in the searches has been both substantial and questionable in effectiveness.

Any examination at all of the plentiful evidence concerning the treatment of POWs and civilian prisoners by NVN provides an immediate unqualified rebuttal of the myth that they were well treated.

---

[35] On occasion they have returned the preserved remains of men of whom they had previously denied having any knowledge.

Myth #14- The determination of the North to carry the war on was never affected by any military setbacks or US actions

The interviews given, and memoirs published, by various individuals who were VC/NVA/NLF/committed communists during the war have revealed that General Giap considered Tet a stunning disaster, that the VC were unable to recruit sufficient replacements afterwards, and that the terrible losses of the '72 invasion caused consternation in the politburo. Dissent was not tolerated in NVN, but the appearance of editorials in the papers there after the '72 retreat, castigating those who were not sufficiently supportive of the government, demonstrates that there was concern in the politburo about an undercurrent of pessimism regarding continuation of the war.

After the Easter Offensive had been repulsed, secret negotiations began between Henry Kissinger and Le Duc Tho, which were clearly a result of that major defeat of the NVA. Eventually they became public and were conducted in Paris, and by October a general agreement was reached. The US stopped all bombing of the North as part of a goodwill gesture while the final agreement was to be worked out.

However, no further progress was made and the Paris discussions turned into an exercise in futility as the communists stalled; finally, the negotiations broke down. By mid-December President Nixon had reached a peak of frustration, and was apprehensive that when Congress reconvened, his powers to conduct the war would be limited. He then decided to unleash the full force[36] of US airpower on NVN as a means to impress the communists

---

[36] Up until then there had been tight restrictions on what could be bombed. Hanoi, Haiphong, SAM storage sites, power generating plants, and other key facilities had been off-limits.

and bring them back to the negotiating table with a more cooperative attitude.

The result was the bombing campaign of NVN known as Linebacker II (sometimes referred to as the Christmas bombings). Starting December 18th, wave after wave of B-52 bombers and other warplanes dropped a total of 40,000 tons of explosives on facilities in and around Hanoi and Haiphong.[37] The devastation of the target areas was enormous, 80% of the electrical grid was smashed, eight major railroad yards were put out of commission, and most of the stored SAM inventory was destroyed. By the 11th day of bombing the supply of SAM missiles was almost totally exhausted, antiaircraft ammunition was in short supply, and the ability of NVN to defend against air attack had deteriorated very badly.

The North Vietnamese leadership then requested a resumption of the negotiations, and the bombing was called off. Agreement was reached on finalizing the Paris Accords, in very much the same form as the US had proposed in October.

The impact of the bombings was massive, the American POWs in Hanoi had rejoiced when the walls of the prison shook, and their guards had shown great fear. Their treatment changed very suddenly for the better, and none of them was ever tortured again. They saw firsthand how much the power of the rain of explosives and the resulting damage impressed their captors.

There is no doubt that the application of focused and effective strategic bombing forced the NVN leadership to return to the negotiations and accept the terms they had previously rejected. They were not fools, and when faced

---

[37] Targeting and delivery was so accurate that there were only ~1600 civilian casualties. In Dresden, 1/4 of this bomb weight had killed over 30K Germans.

with escalating levels of damage to their country's infrastructure, they adapted their actions to avoid a continuation of destruction.[38] Their "invincible will" to fight did not pass the final test, and is simply another myth, albeit a romantic one to which many antiwar activists were emotionally attached.

Myth #15- The United States fought and lost a war in Viet Nam (which was unwinnable in any case)

This is an interesting position to take, since as a general rule a substantially more powerful military power can always conquer a lesser over time, given the will to do so. Although limited wars are common in history, the trend towards total war in which one or both sides apply all or almost all their resources to destroy their enemy goes back in America to the Civil War, and reached a height during WW2. However, the US did not take a total war approach in Viet Nam, or even close to it.

First, a total war approach would have required, as it did in Korea, a strategy that included invading the North. This was never even considered, in part because that might have brought Chinese intervention, as in Korea.

But in even a limited war effort to just cripple NVN and destroy their will to continue supporting conflict in the South, the US could have mined all the harbors of NVN, demolished all rail links and bridges linking them to China, broken all the major dikes protecting essential farmland, adopted a policy of hot pursuit and taken the war to the refuges in Laos and Cambodia, used punitive bombing of major cities and industrial centers (see

---

[38] Many military strategists believe that the use of this kind of airpower much earlier in the war would have had a profound effect on the final outcome, and that the micromanagement of military strategy by the White House was extremely counterproductive to the conduct of the war.

above), and even launched an amphibious invasion north of the DMZ to cut across all the routes into SVN.

Once supplies from China and the Soviet Bloc were cut off and the impact of major damage to the production and transport sectors of the NVN economy was felt, the North Vietnamese would simply not have been able to prosecute the war in the South. They would have undoubtedly marshaled all the forces possible to prevent their own fall from power, but the US could have left their regions by then and SVN would have been stabilized without too much further difficulty once there was no support at all available from the North.

However, whether or not the US would have taken such strong steps is certainly debatable, but it is not necessary to enter that debate; the point is that the US could certainly have won a war with NVN, had the US decided to truly wage war against them as a country.

Antiwar activists have since interpreted the supposed military defeat of a world superpower by a small Asian nation as evidence of the moral superiority of the communist cause, the unconquerable will of those in a just cause, loss of effectiveness by the US military due to resistance within its ranks, and other idealistic/romantic notions. None of these actually applies, but the legacy of these false ideas has had negative effects on thinking about how the US can function in the world.

If, however, the actual strategic goals of the US are examined, we see they could be stated as:
1. prevent the imminent collapse of SVN as it was in 1965;

2. do whatever necessary to stabilize the military and political situations in SVN[39] and help their military become more effective;
3. as the South Vietnamese military grows in size and skill, turn over the conduct of the conflict to them;
4. disengage the bulk of US soldiers from the war, leaving its further waging to a SVN military capable of defending their own country.

The injection of US forces into Viet Nam in 1965 did prevent the collapse of the government, and the heavy involvement of the US military from then through 1970 held the line against the VC/NVA incursions while the South Vietnamese forces did improve and support for the government (or against the communists, depending on how one looks at it) increased. By late 1971 the cities of SVN were reasonably safe, VC activity had diminished sharply, many rural areas had been pacified, and much of the serious combat was against NVA troops, and took place in regions well away from population centers.

Vietnamization did take place successfully, and the forces of SVN wrested a hard-won but undeniable victory against the invading NVA in their Easter Offensive of 1972. There could be no clearer demonstration that the South Vietnamese could, with proper material support, defend themselves.

Accordingly, the war as fought by the US, had been won. All that remained was to provide the SVN forces the support necessary to maintain their strength and effectiveness. The US goals had been met, and the demonstrated capability of SVN to defend itself disproves the myth of the unwinnable war.

---

[39] It must be noted that the absorption of SVN was only the first step in a communist strategy of expansion into Southeast Asia; there were communist insurgencies in Laos and Cambodia supported by NVN, China, and Russia.

Tragically, as political pressures mounted, due to the antiwar campaign and the almost compulsive drive of many Americans to put the war behind them, Congress reduced support to SVN to a fatally low level. Simultaneously, severe restrictions were placed on any direct military actions there by US forces. At the same time, Chinese and Soviet Bloc support to NVN was expanding greatly, so the balance of military power, in terms of weapons, munitions, and equipment, swung far in the direction of the communists.

When the NVA invaded again in 1975, in another 3-pronged attack[40], they did so with new Soviet tanks, trucks, artillery, and SAMs, using 20 of the army's 22 divisions to storm into the South much as the German Army had stormed into France in WW2. Spread across the country and short of much critical materiel (e.g. fuel, ammunition, medical supplies), the SVN forces could not effectively resist the blitzkrieg without the aerial support of US warplanes to blunt the drive; and that support had been forbidden by Congress. Despite the many brave and ultimately fatal stands made by ARVN units (see above), once a retreat was called by President Thieu the situation deteriorated rapidly and finally surrender was no longer avoidable.

---

[40] This was a massive force of 400,000, in contrast to the 200,000 of the 1972 invasion, or the 84,000 of the Tet offensive.

Section 4- The Aftermath

Myth #16- After NVN "liberated" the South, everything went well and suffering ended

When the American forces left the war to the South Vietnamese, there were celebrations in all the antiwar groups, and a general feeling of relief among the American people. The relief was not because everyone identified with the antiwar campaign or was happy with the situation in Viet Nam, but more because it was an end of sorts, a surcease from the constant tension and conflict of those years. By that time, the Civil Rights movement had achieved its major goals, Women's Rights were also recognized, and therefore the great bulk of the fiery causes that had kept the country in ferment had calmed down.

There was a great deal of satisfaction on the part of activists who'd worked for all the movements, as is entirely natural when victory in good causes is obtained after years of struggle. The war protesters perhaps even more than others took pride in their accomplishments. For the media the practice of holding the government and military highly suspect, and not examining events too closely that might contradict the views held by reformers/protesters, became standard practice.

Thus, all the negative events in SE Asia that followed the fall of Saigon received much less close examination than anything that occurred before then.

But what took place in SVN was vindictive retribution and heavy-handed imposition of the communist system, including major repression of human rights. From the needless injuries and deaths of thousands of refugees run over or shelled on the roads as the NVA raced to Saigon, to the subsequent executions of 60-70,000 people and the imprisonment of 800,000 more in concentration camps[41], to the bulldozing of all the military cemeteries of the Southern forces[42], the year following the fall of Saigon was a reign of terror in what had been South Viet Nam. The renaming of Saigon as Ho Chi Minh City would be analogous to the Union renaming Richmond as Lincolnville at the end of the Civil War, and made it clear to the southerners that rather than being liberated, they were a conquered people.

The camps were termed "re-education" camps, and held a wide variety of people, including former SVN military, politicians, public figures, civil servants, religious leaders, and even some former VC/NLF supporters. Within three years about two-thirds of these detainees were released, but the remaining 300,000 or so were kept in captivity for up to 17-18 years. As many as 80,000-90,000 people died in the camps from malnutrition, overwork, disease, and brutal treatment. Very little note was taken of any of this by the US or international press, which during the war had so zealously examined every incident of harm to civilians, etc, attributed to Americans, and every claim of corruption, error, or inefficiency on the part of SVN. And from the antiwar organizations in the US and elsewhere, the silence was deafening.[43]

As time wore on, the unmistakable evidence of how repressive life was under the communists mounted. The exodus of "boat people" and those who fled across Laos and Cambodia to Thailand amounted to perhaps 2 million people, and included not just refugees from the South,

---

[41] For example, the ARVN commanding general from the battle of Xuan Loc spent 17 years in prison for merely doing his duty as a soldier.

[42] Destroying a cemetery in a culture that venerates ancestors is an act of such cruelty and contempt as most Westerners cannot fully appreciate.

[43] A few antiwar figures, including folksinger Joan Baez, did take out a full page ad in the NY Times protesting the treatment of the South by the conquering North, but it garnered no attention, or support from their former comrades.

but also a significant number from the North. Given the strong ties of the culture to the land, and the known dangers of attempted flight[44], having something like 6-7% of the population leave is the clearest and most dramatic evidence imaginable of the ordeals imposed on them.

Amidst the great mass of evidence of the oppression and brutality of the communist regime, two more points stand out. First, during the war years, among the most dramatic and highly publicized incidents were the self-immolations of Buddhist monks. However, more Buddhists burned themselves to death in protest after 1975 than before.[45] Secondly, a number of former NLF/VC dignitaries were among the refugees after 1975, including some high-ranking Northerners who had belonged to the Communist Party and served with the NVA. These were people who had been totally disillusioned by the reality of what amounted to an occupation of the South by the North, and the implementation of a dysfunctional socialist system that dropped the standard of living in the unified Viet Nam to the lowest in SE Asia (despite receiving several billion dollars yearly in aid from the Soviet Bloc).

While there was notice of the "boat people" by the media, since their appearance at numerous ports in the region was impossible to ignore, oddly enough there was comparatively little discussion of why this exodus was taking place. Nor were the defections of former communists, the suppression of human rights[46], or the terrible conditions of the "re-education" camps subjects of any coverage by major news organizations. Viet Nam

---

[44] Deaths of boat people due to pirates, weather, etc, have been estimated to approach 50%.

[45] A full dozen immolated themselves in one incident in November 1975, and the most recent immolation took place in December, 2003.

[46] Freedom of speech vanished and religious freedom was severely curtailed, among other things.

and China waged a brief but intense conflict, Viet Nam sent divisions into Cambodia and colonized territory there, Viet Nam engaged in ruthless suppression of the Montagnard peoples, but none of these events made any headlines. It was as if Viet Nam and the immediate vicinity had become as interesting to the media as Tierra del Fuego or the Solomon Islands.

Under the politburo no dissent is tolerated, and a long list of suppressed/persecuted dissidents might start with:

Nguyen Chi Thien, the most famous living VN poet, a Northerner and originally a supporter of Ho, who spent 25 years in prison for criticizing the Hanoi regime;

Nguyen Khac Toan, an NVA war veteran who became a freelance writer and reporter, describing citizen protests and agitating on behalf of other veterans for reform, given a 12 year sentence after a 1-day trial for "espionage";

Nguyen Dinh Huy, history professor in Saigon, jailed for 17 years after the war's end, he then started a pro-democracy movement, was held without trial for 2 years, then sentenced to 15 years in a closed trial.

Duong Quynh Hoa, a communist from her youth, founding member of the NLF, and high Party official, who became disillusioned with corruption, resigned her Party membership, and became severely critical of the regime.

Most Venerable Thich Huyen Quang, 86 year old leader of the United Buddhist Church of Viet Nam, who has spent over 20 years under house arrest for protesting the repression of the UBCV.

The amazing lack of publicity on life under the communists enabled those who wished it to hang on to the comfortable myth that the fall of Saigon had brought peace, harmony, and social justice to the country.

Myth #17- The Domino Theory was a silly invention, and nothing remotely positive resulted from US involvement in Viet Nam

In the first place, Laos and Cambodia, already long under attack by communist groups, were doomed by the fall of South Viet Nam. The result in Cambodia of the communist takeover under Pol Pot was one of the most terrible events of the 20th century, the slaughter of almost 25% of the nation's entire population, plus long lasting damage to the social structure due to the loss of so many people with critical skills (doctors, educators, technicians, etc.). Laos today is still ruled by communists, with a low standard of living and lack of personal freedoms.

Aside from any predictions by US diplomats, politicians, or intelligence agencies, the leaders of Thailand, Malaysia, and Singapore expressed clear concerns before and during the war about the likelihood that the rapid abandonment of Viet Nam to the communists would bring their nations into peril. The length of the war and the massive population drain left North Viet Nam exhausted, and concentrating on the takeover of the South. A subsequent adventure in Cambodia and finally a falling out with China eradicated any desire or capacity to promulgate communism into the rest of SE Asia.

Further, the vast expenditures the Soviets made in supporting NVN throughout and after the war put a major strain on Moscow's economy. The subsequent Russian invasion of Afghanistan and the years of losses there added much more difficulty to the maintenance of the Soviet empire, and it finally collapsed. The investment they had made in Viet Nam contributed to a significant degree to that succession of events.

Therefore, the Domino Theory certainly cannot be proven invalid, and the fact that some good was accomplished for the remaining free nations of SE Asia, and possibly the end of the Cold War, through the blood and sacrifice of the US in Viet Nam is clear. The claims to the contrary, while again a comforting thought for those who opposed the war, must be seen as myths too.

Section 5- Summary Comments

The underlying causes of the war in Viet Nam go all the way back to French colonial policy of the 19th century and the transport of Vladimir Lenin into Russia by the Germans in 1917. Ultimately those events led to the complex situation faced by the US in the early 1960s, which had effects over much of SE Asia, some of which continue to the present time.

The famous quote "A little learning is a dangerous thing" applies perfectly to any attempt to study the pattern of conflicts in that region. Achieving any significant level of understanding of the myriad factors operating there from 1945 through 1990 takes years of study, and casual study of the US involvement in Viet Nam from 1965 to 1975 has promoted much more misunderstanding than valid learning. The massive amount of misinformation about the war and its aftermath, couched in a large collection of myths that appear not just in rumor and folklore, but in many scholarly books, reports, articles, and documentaries, lies in wait for the inquiring student like a giant swamp with lots of quicksand.

The dangers of enshrining myths relate indirectly to the famous quote by George Santayana - "Those who fail to learn the lessons of history are doomed to repeat them." A corollary to that is "Those who embrace the false lessons of psuedohistory are condemned to march into self-made disasters, which they will be unable to comprehend until far too late".

Accepting the myths of Viet Nam has led many people to readily accept ideas such as:
1. any military action by the US outside its borders is almost certain to turn into a "quagmire";

2. the US and international media are free of bias and sensationalism in their reporting of US actions and their results;

3. antiwar activists are always knowledgeable and their ideas are bound to shorten conflict and save lives; and

4. the exposure of any incident in which US military may have acted inappropriately is ample proof that the entire venture is morally wrong and inherently incapable of bringing about anything positive.

The ultimate effect of beliefs like these and others related to the myths of Viet Nam, should their influence become prevalent in Congress, would be to leave the USA essentially paralyzed among the nations of the world. This would serve no one except those movements and nations that wish to conquer or subvert others, and those whose policies are repressive and cruel. This is why it is important to study Viet Nam carefully, to determine what the true lessons are from that conflict.

The attached bibliography consists of those works that a distinguished board of Viet Nam veterans, writers, and historians consider at least reasonably accurate and with minimal bias. There are also numerous websites listed where the researcher can find much valuable information relating to the war and subsequent events.

Lastly, everyone should recognize that there are several classes of obvious victims of the war, starting with all the Vietnamese who died or suffered terribly as part of it (including not just the Southerners, but also the great majority of Northerners who served in the war, whether drafted or by sincere belief in the liberation of the South). There are the millions of Vietnamese refugees who felt compelled to leave their country and start life anew in foreign lands, and those who remained in Viet Nam but who find life under communism onerous. There are all those who suffered and died in Laos and

Cambodia as part of the communist Indochina war. There are all the Americans, Australians, New Zealanders, Koreans, Canadians, Thais, and others who fought and died in attempting to help SVN. And then there are those who served in the war but survived, though not without scars, some of which are visible, some of which are not.

Without being overly partisan, the authors wish to honor all the victims by trying to help those who wish to learn about them recognize and avoid the patches of quicksand that are the myths of Viet Nam.

Recommended Reading

The following are a selection from the many books to be found that deal with the war on various levels. Some are well known classics (e.g. the famous Bernard Fall work), others are excellent but less known (Douglas Pike's books), and some are not commonly found or easy to obtain. Many of these books do deal directly with some of the myths enumerated above, but the bulk of them are provided as valuable references for anyone wishing to research the war while avoiding the frequent inaccuracies and misstatements found in too many popular sources. (A few volumes of special worth are marked *)

INTRODUCTION

1. **The Two Viet-Nams**; Bernard Fall; Frederick A Praeger, NY; 1963 [*The definitive comparison of North and South Viet Nam up to the early 1960s*]

2. **North Viet Nam Today- Profile of a Communist Satellite**; edited by P.J. Honey; Frederick A. Praeger, NY; 1962

3. **Communism in North Viet Nam**; P.J. Honey; MIT Press, Cambridge, MA; 1963

4. **Advice and Support: The Early Years, 1941-1960**; Ronald H. Spector; US Government Printing Office; 1983

5. **Government and Revolution**; Dennis J. Duncanson; Oxford University Press, New York/London; 1968

6. **The Lost Revolution**; Robert Shaplen; Harper-Colophon; 1966 [*Reporter and expert on SE Asia enumerates US policy errors, omissions, and general clumsiness*]

7. **Why We Were In Vietnam**; Norman Podhoretz; Simon and Schuster, NY; 1983

8. **Vietnam: The Necessary War**; Michael Lind; The Free Press, NY; 1999 [Chapters 3 and 8 are not recommended.]

THE ENEMY

9. **Portrait of the Enemy**; David Chanoff & Doan Van Toai; Random House, NY; 1986 [*unique compilation of individual VC/NVA views, some of them surprising and informative*]

10. ***A Viet Cong Memoir**; Truong Nhu Tang with David Chanoff and Doan Van Toai; Harcourt Brace Jovanovich, NY; 1985 [*caustic commentary by a former NLF official*]

11. **Primer for Revolt**; Truong Chinh; Praeger, NY; 1963 [*strategic plan used against the French, applied as well against Saigon and Washington*]

12. **Inside the VC and the NVA: The Real Story of North Vietnam's Armed Forces**; Michael Lee Lanning and Dan Cragg; Ballatine Books, NY; 1992

13. ***Viet Cong: The Organization and Techniques of the National Liberation Front of South Vietnam**; Douglas Pike; MIT Press, Cambridge, MA; 1966 [*the definitive analysis of the VC in their heyday*]

14. **The Communist Insurgent Infrastructure in South Vietnam: A Study of Organization and Strategy**; Michael Charles Conley; The American University, Washington, DC; 1966 [*clear explanation of VC/NLF organization, tactics, and propaganda*]

15. **PAVN: People's Army of Vietnam**; Douglas Pike; Da Capo Press, NY; 1986

16. **Vietnam and the Soviet Union: Anatomy of an Alliance**; Douglas Pike; Westview Press, Boulder, CO; 1987

17. **History of Vietnamese Communism, 1925-1976**; Douglas Pike; Hoover Institution Press, Stanford, CA; 1978

18. ***Communism in Southeast Asia**; Justus M. van der Kroef; University of California Press, Berkley, CA; 1980 [*underscores validity of the Domino Theory and volatility of Southeast Asia*]

19. **Viet Namese Communism – Its Origin and Development**; Robert F. Turner; Hoover Institution Press, Stanford, CA; 1975 [*a superb dissection of VN communists, their strategies and practices*]

20. ***Ho Chi Minh, A Life**; William S. Duiker; Hyperion, NY; 2000 [*frank examination of the life & works of "Uncle Ho"*]

21. **Vision Accomplished? The Enigma of Ho Chi Minh**; N. Khac Huyen; Collier Books, NY; 1971 [*his rise to power and the tactics he used to accomplish it*]

THE STRATEGY

22. **Protracted Conflict: A Challenging Study of Communist Strategy**; Robert Strausz Hupe, William Kinter, James Dougherty, and Alvin Cottrell; Harper & Row, NY; 1963 [*a history of effective communist strategies and ineffective US counters, with some applications in VN*]

23. **Dereliction of Duty: Lyndon Johnson, Robert McNamara, the Joint Chiefs of Staff, and the Lies That Led to Vietnam**; H. R. McMaster; HarperCollins, NY; 1997 [*shows how McNamara's inputs damaged US efforts in VN*]

24. ***Peace Is Not At Hand**; Sir Robert Thompson; David McKay Company Inc., NY; 1974

25. **A Soldier Reports**; William C. Westmoreland; Doubleday, NY; 1976 [*a key contribution on the war*]

26. ***Vietnam: Strategy for a Stalemate**; F. Charles Parker, IV; Paragon House, NY; 1989 [*thoroughly researched book detailing McNamara's total failure as a strategist*]

27. **Strategy For Defeat: Vietnam in Retrospect**; U. S. Grant Sharp; Presidio Press, San Rafael, CA; 1978

28. **The Key to Failure: Laos and the Vietnam War**; Norman Hannah; Madison Books, Lanham, MD; 1987 [*a unique scrutiny of the critical failure to cut the Ho Chi Minh Trail*]

29. ***On Strategy: A Critical Analysis of the Vietnam War**; Harry Summers; Presidio Press, Novato, CA; 1982 [*key exposition of the grossly flawed US strategy in the war*]

THE MEDIA WAR

30. ***News From Nowhere: Television and the News**; Edward J. Epstein; Random House, NY; 1973; *Vietnam War*; pp xi-xix, 9-19, 22, 25-29, 33, 43, 183, 187, 211-213, 248-251 [*stinging indictment of media focus on drama and ratings over substance*]

31. **Anti-Americanism: Critiques at Home and Abroad, 1965-1990**; Paul Hollander; Oxford University Press, NY; 1992; Chap. 4, *Mass Media*, pp 215-255

32. **Covert Cadre: Inside the Institute for Policy Studies**; Steven Powell; Green Hill Publishing, Ottawa, IL; 1987; Chap. 2, *IPS and the Major Media*, pp 23-24; Chap. 3, *Influencing the Media on Vietnam*, pp 33-43; Chaps 8, 9, 10, *IPS and the Media*, pp 101-163; Appendix 4, *IPS and the Media*, p 372

33. **How to Lose a War**; Robert Elegant; Ethics and Public Policy Center, Washington, DC; April, 1982 (reprint of an article in the British journal *Encounter*, August, 1981) [*an experienced reporter's commentary on the failures of the media during the war*] (available on the Viet-Myths website)

34. ***Big Story: How the American Press and Television Reported and Interpreted the Crisis of Tet 1968 in Vietnam and Washington**; Peter Braestrup; Presidio Press, Novato, CA; 1994 [*penetrating analysis of the media's depiction of the Tet Offensive and its meaning*]

35. **Losers Are Pirates: A Close Look at the PBS Series "Vietnam: A Television History"**(revised edition); James Banerian; Sphinx Publishing Company, Phoenix, AZ; 1985 [*incisive dissection of the PBS series and its defects*]

36. **Vietnam at the Movies**; Michael Lee Lanning; Fawcett Columbine, NY; 1994

THE POLITICAL WAR

37. **Dezinformatsia: Active Measures in Soviet Strategy**; Richard H. Shultz and Roy Godson; Pergamon-Brassey's, NY; 1984; *Vietnam War*, pp vii-x, 54-57, 60, 63-66, 124-126, 181-182

38. ***Target America: The Influence of Communist Propaganda on U.S. Media**; James Tyson; Regnery gateway, NY; 1988 [*detailed examination of the propaganda campaign waged during the war*]

39. **Deconstructing the Left: From Vietnam to the Persian Gulf**; Peter Collier and David Horowitz; Second Thoughts Books, Lanham, MD; 1991; Part. II, Chap 1; *My Vietnam Lessons*, pp 78-85; Part III, Chap. 2; *Student Activists;*

Then and Now, pp 131-138; Part IV, Chap 3; *The "Peace" Movement*, pp 185-191

40. ***Radical Son: A Journey Through Our Times**; David Horowitz; The Free Press, NY; 1997; Part 4, *Revolutions (1968-1973)*, pp 155-202 [*renowned former antiwar leftist recounts his evolution from communism into conservatism*]

41. **Communism and the New Left: What They're Up To Now**; (anon); Books by U.S. News and World Report; Washington, DC; 1969; Chap. 2; *How They Exploit War*, pp 41-64

42. **Congressional Record**; Proceedings and Debates of the 92nd Congress; First Session; April 21, 1971; *The Second Front of the Vietnam War: Communist Subversion in the Peace Movement*; report by Hon. John G. Schmitz, Hon. Fletcher Thompson, and Hon. Roger H. Zion; House Internal Security Committee; published in paperback as **The Viet Cong Front in the United States** with subject headings and glossary; Western Islands, Belmont, MA; (no date).

43. **Betrayal in Vietnam**; Louis A. Fanning; Arlington House, New Rochelle, NY; 1976

THE UNCONVENTIONAL WAR

44. **The Secret War Against Hanoi: Kennedy's and Johnson's Use of Spies, Saboteurs, and Covert Warriors in North Vietnam**; Richard Shultz; Harper Collins, NY; 1999

45. **Phoenix and the Birds of Prey: The CIA's Secret Campaign to Destroy the Viet Cong**; Mark Moyer; Naval Institute Press, Annapolis, MD; 1997 [*insightful expose of "the official assassination program" which never existed*]

46. **Green Berets at War: U.S. Army Special Forces in Southeast Asia, 1956–1975**; Shelby L. Stanton; Presidio Press, Novato, CA; 1985

47. **SOG: The Secret Wars of America's Commandos in Vietnam**; John L. Plaster; Simon & Schuster, NY; 1997 [*chronicles special tactics and skills used by Green Berets*]

THE CONVENTIONAL WAR

48. **Historical Atlas of the Vietnam War**; Harry Summers; Houghton Mifflin, NY; 1995

49. **Vietnam: The Decisive Battles**; John Pimlott; Macmillan; NY; 1990.

50. **Battlefront Vietnam: How the War Was Really Fought**; Tom Carhart; Warner Books, NY; 1984

51. **The 25-Year War: America's Military Role in Vietnam**; Bruce Palmer, Jr.; The University Press of Kentucky. Lexington, KY; 1984

52. **Summons of the Trumpet: A History of the Vietnam War From A Military Man's Viewpoint**; Dave Richard Palmer; Presidio Press, Novato, CA; 1978

53. ***Vietnam At War: The History, 1946-1975**; Phillip Davidson,; Oxford University Press, NY; 1988 [*considered by some to be the single best military account of the war*]

54. ***A Better War: The Unexamined Victories and Final Tragedy of America's Last Years in Vietnam**; Lewis Sorley; Harcourt, Inc., NY; 1999 [*a collection of important facts about the war in the 1969-1975 period*]

55. **The Rise & Fall of an American Army: U.S. Ground Forces in Vietnam, 1965-1973**; Shelby Stanton; Presidio Press, Novato, CA; 1985

56. ***Unheralded Victory**; Mark W. Woodruff; Vandamere Press, Arlington, VA; 1999

THE COMBAT

57. **Vietnam: A Reader from the Pages of Vietnam Magazine**; David T. Zabecki (ed.); ibooks, NY; 2002

58. **The Soldiers' Story: Vietnam in Their Own Words**; Ron Steinman; TV Books, NY; 1999

59. **A Life in a Year: The American Infantryman in Vietnam, 1965–1972**; James R. Ebert; Presidio Press, Novato, CA; 1993

60. **A Distant Challenge: The US Infantryman in Vietnam, 1967-1972**; Infantry Magazine, Albert N. Garland (ed.); The Battery Press, Nashville, TN; 1983

61. ***No Shining Armor: The Marines at War in Vietnam, an Oral History**; Otto J. Lehrack; University Press of Kansas; Lawrence, KA; 1992 [*excellent wide-ranging collection of interviews with Marine officers and enlisted*]

62. **Rice Paddy Grunt**; John M.G. Brown; Regnery Gateway, Lake Bluff, IL; 1986

63. ***To Bear Any Burden: The Vietnam War and Its Aftermath in the Words of Americans and Southeast Asians**; Santoli, Al, ed.;   Dutton, New York; 1985 (reprinted 2003 by Indiana University Press) [*outstanding oral history from many viewpoints, including postwar*]

64. **On Point, A Rifleman's Year in the Boonies**; Roger Hayes; Presidio Press, California; 2000

THE AFTERMATH

65. ***The Vietnamese Gulag**; Doan Van Toai and David Chanoff; Simon & Schuster, NY; 1986 [*ample documentation of the communist gulag created after 1975*]

66. **Reeducation in Post Vietnam: Personal Postscripts to Peace**; Edward Metzner; Texas A&M Press, College Station, TX; 2001

67. **Vietnam Under Communism**; Nguyen Van Canh; Hoover Institution, Palo Alto, CA; 1983 [*the inefficiency, injustice, and repression of the VN police state after 1975*]

ADVISORY ACCOUNTS

68. **The Advisor**; John Cook; Bantam Books, NY; 1987 (previously published by Dorrance, 1973) [*an advisor's history of his tour and its successes*]

69. **Combat Recon- My Year With The ARVN**; Robert D. Parrish; St. Martin's Press, NY; 1991 [*detailed account of an advisor and his SVN partners, demonstrating the will and capability of the ARVN to fight*]

70. ***Silence Was A Weapon**; Stuart A. Herrington; Presidio Press, Novato, CA; 1982 (retitled Stalking the Viet Cong

about 1995) [*candid chronicle of successes and failures from an advisor who spoke the language and knew Vietnamese from both sides of the conflict*]

71. **Once A Warrior King**; David Donovan; McGraw-Hill Books, NY;1985 [*the bonding of an advisor to the South Vietnamese and their struggle, and his reactions to flawed strategies imposed by Washington*]

EVALUATIONS

72. **Lost Victory: A Firsthand Account of America's Sixteen-Year Involvement in Vietnam**; William Colby; Contemporary Books, Chicago, 1989

73. ***America in Vietnam**; Guenter Lewy; Oxford University Press, NY; 1978 [*an informative book of unusual scope, probing many controversial aspects of the war*]

74. **Stolen Valor: How the Vietnam Generation Was Robbed of its Heroes and its History**; B. G. Burkett & Glenna Whitley; Verity Press, Dallas, TX; 1998; Chapters 5, 6, 8, 9, and 13 through 24 [chapters 1, 2, 3, and 4 are optional [*fully documented expose of myths regarding Vietvets and the shocking incidence of phony "war heroes"*]

75. ***The 25-Year Century: A South Vietnamese General Remembers the Indochina War to the Fall of Saigon**; Lam Quang Thi; University of North Texas Press, Denton, TX; 2002 [a *candid review of the war with some surprising conclusions*]

76. **The War Managers: American Generals Reflect on Vietnam**; Douglas Kinnard; Da Capo Press, NY; 1991

77. **Vietnam As History: Ten Years After the Paris Peace Accords**; Peter Braestrup (ed.); University Press of America, Washington, DC; 1981

78. **The Real Lessons of the Vietnam War: Reflections 25 Years After the Fall of Saigon**; John N. Moore and Robert F. Turner; Carolina Academic Press, Durham, NC; 2002

SOUTH VIETNAMESE ACCOUNTS

79. **Where the Orange Blooms**; Thomas Taylor; McGraw-Hill, NY; 1989 [*fascinating story of a SVN interpreter for the US 101st Div, later in the ARVN, finally his imprisonment and postwar life in SVN*]

80. **Hope and Vanished Reality**; Nguyen Xuan Phong; Xlibris.com, Philadelphia; 2002

81. **The Inviting Call of Wandering Souls: Memoir of an ARVN Liaison Officer to the United States Forces in Vietnam Who Was Imprisoned in Communist Re-eduction Camps and Then Escaped**; Lu Van Thanh; McFarland, Jefferson, N.C.; 1997

82. ***The Will of Heaven: A Story of One Vietnamese and the End of His World**; Nguyen Ngoc Ngan and E. E. Richie; Dutton, New York; 1982 [*detailed account by a SVN officer of defeat, the re-education camp, his escape, and postwar life in the South*]

83. **In the Jaws of History**; Bui Diem with David Chanoff,. Houghton Mifflin, Boston; 1987

POW ACCOUNTS

84. **In Love and War**; Jim and Sybil Stockdale; Harper & Row Publishers , New York; 1984 [*from one of the best-known POWs, including details of his wife's experiences during his incarceration*]

85. **Five Years to Freedom**; James N. Rowe; Little, Brown & Company, Boston, MA; 1971 [*unique account by a man who spoke Vietnamese and interacted with both VC and NVA captors*]

86. ***P.O.W., A Definitive History of the American Prisoner of War Experience in Viet Nam, 1964-1973**; John G. Hubbell; Reader' Digest Press, distributed by Thomas Y. Crowell Company; 1976

87. **Honor Bound: American Prisoners of War in Southeast Asia, 1961-1973**; Stuart Rochester & Frederick Kiley; Naval Institute Press, Annapolis, MD; 1999

88. **Leave No Man Behind**; Garnett Bell with George J. Veith; Goblin Fern Press, Madison, WI; 2004

CAP Marines [one example of a US/SVN program that operated successfully on village level to combat the VC]

89. **The Village**; Francis West; University of Wisconsin Press, Madison; 1985

90. ***A Personal War In Viet Nam**; Robert Flynn; Texas A & M Press ; College Station, TX; 1989

91. **A Field of Innocence**; Jack Estes; Breitenbush Books, Portland, OR; 1987 [*contains an absorbing history of the author's changes in thought and commitment during his service*]

REFERENCES

92. **Vietnam War Almanac**; Harry Summers; Facts On File, NY, 1985

93. **Vietnam War Diary: 1964-1975**; Charles Bishop (ed.); The Military Press; NY; 1990

94. **The World Almanac of the Vietnam War**; John Bowman (ed.); Bison Books, NY; 1985

95. **A Wider War**; Donald Kirk; Praeger Publishers, NY;1971 [*The above book is unique insofar as it deals with the countries adjacent to RVN and NVN, Laos, Cambodia, and Thailand, detailing Hanoi-sponsored wars in each.*]

96. **Tragic Mountains**; Jane Hamilton-Merritt; Indiana University Press, IN: 1993 [*Compelling story of the Hmong peoples in the aftermath of the war.*]

WEBSITES OF INTEREST

Sites run by Viet Nam Veterans

Viet-Myths.net
a site rich with numerous lectures and articles by some of the most knowledgeable people in the field

vietnamlegacy.org
founded in May 2005 by a panel of distinguished veterans in order to distinguish truth from fiction

VIET NAM

fva.org
documents Hanoi human rights violations.

danchu.net
information on Buddhist sites. Documents Hanoi past and present crackdown on Hoa Hao and others

crfvn.org
Committee for Religious Freedom in VN.

Montagnard-Foundation.org
Montagnard history, present situation and oppression.

Generalhieu.com
Memorial website for the late RVNAF Gen. Nguyen Van Hieu, held in honor by many former SVN military

Caodai.net
dedicated to Cao Dai Religion, Hanoi mistreatment of same

vnhrnet.org
Viet Nam Human Rights Net

vnaf.net
VN air force, has good historical info

HUMAN RIGHTS ORGANIZATIONS

Amnestyusa.org
Amnesty International. Type in "Viet Nam" or "Laos" or "Cambodia" in search box)

hrw.org
(Human Rights Watch with search box for different countries)

Rsf.org

Reporters Without Frontiers-monitors infringement of press freedom by country

cpj.org
Committee to Protect Journalists   Same as above with slightly different info, studies, etc.

unpo.org
Unrepresented People's Organization, concerned with oppression of ethnic minorities such as Montagnards

ahrchk.net
Asian Human Rights Commission

Phaseloop.com
Lists people imprisoned for political views. Many entries for VN, Laos.

CAMBODIA

Khmerkrom.net	Khmernet.com
Cambodianpolitics.org	Camweb.org
Gocambodia.com	Khmer.org
Cambodiadaily.com	Khmerintelligence.org

LAOS	HMONG
Laoveterans.earthlink.net	Hmongnet.org
Laohumrights@earthlink.net	Hmongnation.com
Vietianetimes.com	Hmongtimes.com
Laodemocracy.com	Neeg.org
Laonews.net	Hmongtoday.com
secretwarinlaos.com	Factfinding.org

Proper use of internet search engines will turn up myriad sites with articles on the war, the literature, the main characters, major events, etc. The researcher is cautioned to check the validity of all inputs to be found there. Many are valuable and accurate, others are subject to at least some inaccuracy/bias, and at least a few contain gross misinformation very nicely presented.